At the Table of the Unknown

At the Table of the Unknown

poems by
Alexandra Umlas

MOON
TIDE PRESS

~2019~

At the Table of the Unknown

Editor-in-chief
Eric Morago

Associate Editors
José Enrique Medina, Michael Miller

Marketing Director
Dania Alkhouli

Marketing Assistant
Ellen Webre

Proofreader
Jim Hoggatt

Front cover art
Angie Rehnberg

Author photo
Sheri DiPietro

Book design
Michael Wada

Moon Tide logo design
Abraham Gomez

At the Table of the Unknown
is published by Moon Tide Press

Moon Tide Press #166
6745 Washington Ave. Whittier, CA 90601
www.moontidepress.com

FIRST EDITION

Printed in the United States of America

ISBN # 978-1-7339493-2-3

Further Praise for *At the Table of the Unknown*. . .

If the *mise-en-scène* of many poems in this debut volume by Alexandra Umlas is domestic, and the prosody traditional, the versification nevertheless belies its suburban context. With an ear attuned to the nuanced placement of the caesura, the empathy of Umlas's imagination encompasses the multitudinous tensions generated within a home, just as happy families turn out, in fact, to be different in their hard-won equanimity, so too do Umlas's poems provide us with a surprising amount of variegated pleasure. Those who admire the nimble dexterity and wisdom of Timothy Steele and A.E. Stallings now have a chance to champion another poet on course to join their company. These poems aren't meant to comfort you, but there is a solace in the way in which they defamiliarize the ostensible reassurances of daily life, and leave us grateful for incremental rewards, not the least of which is this volume of superb poetry.

> — Bill Mohr, author of *The Headwaters of Nirvana* and
> *Holdouts: The Los Angeles Poetry Renaissance 1948-1992*

What joy opening a first poetry collection to find a fully realized, compelling work of art. The terrain of *At the Table of the Unknown* is the predictability and surprise of daily life under the shadow of its possible interruption. I think of Tess Gallagher's essay, "The Poem as a Reservoir for Grief," in which she lauds poetry's ability to return one to the experience of grief in search of its transformation. In "Villanelle for Victor," Alexandra Umlas has found the perfect form for cradling grief and making something from it. In "Work," a crown of sonnets, Umlas gives quotidian life its due: *the work of letting go, the work of loss/ that travels through the body/weaves across/the workings of the heart, the way it cleaves—/that work that gets inside and never leaves. At the Table of the Unknown* is a luminous debut.

> — Donna Hilbert, author of *Gravity: New & Selected Poems*

What makes Alexandra Umlas special as a poet? She has lived widely and packed her poems full of all sorts of details from that life. For an example, see "Work," a chronicle of lousy, financially necessary jobs which she has elevated into the unlikely form of a Crown of Sonnets. What astonishes me is how each page of her collection opens a fresh surprise in form as in content. Alex Umlas has waited long enough and worked hard enough to present us with a brilliant, fully formed book of poems out of a fully shaped life.

— John Ridland, author of *Happy in an Ordinary Thing*

The wisdom lurking in Alexandra Umlas's debut collection *At the Table of the Unknown* is this: *Disaster sits, a winged thing waiting*. Umlas's poems speak to the sublime and the dangerous in every middle-class home, fast food restaurant, schoolroom or tennis court. With a keen eye for detail, Umlas serves up gratitude with a side of mystery. Even the title of the book promises a feast of ambiguity. In this precarious world, cooking a chicken turns into an existential question. Blackberries and beets stain like blood and bruises. Lime trees weep. Mothers are murderers of snails. These poems will stay with you because they are earnest in their existential questions, authentic in their scrutiny of everyday life and combine to create a striking portrait of how *Death and the living sing to each other*.

— Arminé Iknadossian, author of *All That Wasted Fruit*

for Greg, Ella, and Vivienne

Contents

Part 4: Where Life Has Been

Part 5: Disassembling

Part 6: Eyes

Bounty and Loss: The World of Alex Umlas

"It is not everyday that world arranges itself into a poem," wrote Wallace Stevens. His statement speaks to the agency of the world, and either its desire to be a poem, or its willingness to become one at the random hands of fate (if fate can be called random) (or have hands). In the hands of poet Alex Umlas, the world regularly arranges itself. For Umlas, the world becomes a place of small spaces and moments of clarity and beauty, of complex thought willing to be wrangled, of layers willing to be separated and observed the way a tree trunk displays its rings.

Umlas is a poet of the known, the observable, who takes as her mission to tease out the unknown that surrounds and imbues the known with grace, a giftedness of meaning that makes the quotidian manageable and often, remarkable. In this vein, Emily Dickinson's wrote: "It is true that the unknown is the largest need of the intellect, though for it, no one thinks to thank God...". Umlas, like Dickinson, uses her immediate surroundings as material for reveries and revelations about the nature of existence. Dickinson's pudding is Umlas's mangoes, beets, persimmons. Chicken. Aging and mortality find their way, as well, her narrators laden with the responsibilities of being sandwiched between the needs of parent and child, as well as the needs of the self as an artist.

Some poets need to represent the artist as someone removed from the world, removed from the need to earn a living, wipe down a table, drive a carpool, clean a gutter, find a few minutes of peace in a yoga class. For some poets, everyday seems like one long yoga class with interruptions for granola bars, hard liquor, and writing long-hand. One can love those poets (they are getting more rare) but learn to develop a great appreciation for poets who juggle, who multi-task, to answer to many roles, and who try to render this world of detail and task into poems that embrace what painter Ben Shahn called "the shape of content," in his Charles Eliot Norton lectures.

Umlas's comfort with inherited forms (let's not call them traditional – they have been made and remade, torn apart and Frankensteined together, and still, the golden mean of the Italian sonnet, with its turn after the octave, continues to show up in the proportions of a large percentage of free verse – can't we accept a good thing when we see it?) sets her apart from many younger poets. She does not work in these forms begrudgingly – she fabricates her rhyme and meter out of her fealty to the ear's desires, which speak at the behest of the body. She loves the sounds of language and where form leads her more than she trusts the interest-level of her perceptions, and her musical choices compel her to trust her subconscious perceptions (where the bulk of our wisdom lies).

When reading Umlas's poems, one can't help but hear Frost and Plath. The well-made line, the strong pull of the iambic rhythm, an engagement with the natural world and natural speech of Frost find a home in Umlas's poems, along with no small shortage of irony: "Mine is an ordinary life for sure – most would concur," she writes at the beginning of "Ordinary Ends," which concludes with the following: ..."You/know, so do I/that ordinary ends; all good things do." (Frost might/did say, "Provide, provide.") The poem, "Fillet" concludes with a daughter inheriting the father's commonplace wisdom: "You should never/save the best for last – it might not be there/when you are ready for it."

Many a critical essay has been written on domesticity in Sylvia Plath's poetry. I think the best response to the work comes from later poets being inspired and entering into conversation with the earlier poems, and Umlas does just that, displaying appreciation along with unease: how does the voice of the poet emerge amidst the amalgam of tasks, details, requests, and demands involved with being a spouse and a parent? From Plath, Umlas borrows the bravery to adore and fear one's offspring, though the fear mostly comes from the desire to protect them, and the fear that one cannot.

Throughout the collection, the musicality of language prevails, as in the poem, "Peach Stones," which describes a burned-down monastery: "… heavy voices floating, finding refuge/relief, relics/rendering a rest spot/for peace for place for peeling/ the sun's skin back behind the mountain…". The other sustaining value is the importance of making

12

an emotional connection with the reader. Frost wrote, "There are three things, after all, that a poem must reach: the eye, the ear, and what we may call the heart or mind. It is most important of all to reach the heart of the reader." In each poem, Umlas strives for that connection, and when the sound and language play is most dense, the poem works even harder to extend itself, to let the reader know: you matter. Our bond matters. Umlas shapes her content into moments of respite and regret, engagement and distance, doubt and praise. Come to the table, she says. We will figure it out then, and there.

— Patty Seyburn

A Foundation for Writing: Guardrails

Since I was the oldest child of three, the rules that governed our household were freshly built for me, and therefore, very strong. We spent the afternoons after school roaming our circular neighborhood in Long Beach, which was gated with a sliding, metal gate, and had a completely rounded street, so that if you began to walk in any direction, you'd find yourself back where you started, on your own front lawn. There was an omnipresent cyclical nature to the days. The earth spun around the same way as our bicycle wheels in the street or as the clothes spun in the washer. We spun our insular cocoons, our beautifully safe childhoods, so that we could, slowly, eventually, and innocuously, grow into adults.

There was an abandoned building in Long Beach's Bixby Knolls with a tennis court on the roof. I would hop the fence and take the fire escape stairs to the top. It was quiet and smoggy and perfect for writing. My mom cooked a rotation of dinners each week – spaghetti and meatballs with Prego, pot roast, baked chicken, foil-baked orange roughy, fried pork chops, and a night of leftovers. Saturdays or Sundays we would go to Arnold's Family Restaurant, which was cafeteria-style. You chose your main entrée, your vegetable, your bread, and then there was always Jell-O or pudding.

For me, life was predictable; but as I state in my poem, "Ordinary Ends," "I know that ordinary ends; all good things do." This line comes from my realization of the impermanent nature of things. As I became an adult, my favorite place became a monastery halfway up the Santa Ynez Mountains, where at 6:00 am each morning, the Benedictine monks of Mount Calvary began their first morning service, Vigils. Vigils is a simple service. The monks' voices rose out of the small, wood-laden chapel in Santa Barbara with the sun. There was always a thick cloud-cover this early in the morning, so the city of Santa Barbara was hidden from view, and the monastery often seemed to be floating out of a cloud. The Benedictine monks who lived there had vowed to live their life finding the divine in the everyday. It was an astonishingly spiritual, beautiful place. On November 13, 2008, a fire was started in Mar i Cel, an open space preserve in Montecito. Because there is a special tea house on the preserve, the fire was named the "Tea Fire." 210 homes were destroyed. The monastery also burned to the ground. They would never rebuild in that location. In Rebecca Cathcart's *New York Times* article about the monastery, she describes the aftermath of the fire:

> Two small artist's studios near the main building were intact. An icon of Christ that Brother Brown had been painting with pigments made from egg yolk and mineral powder was still on a desk. A cello sat a few feet away, unharmed. In the chaos of wind and fire, a sheriff's deputy had moved another monk's telescope outside, where it remained unscathed.
>
> "In the midst of all this destruction," Brother Brown, 46, said Tuesday, "miracles happened all over the place."

The monastery still lives clearly in my imagination, and yet it is gone. It is a place that is both everlasting and temporary. I have found I can live better with the experience and pain of loss, of many kinds of loss, with poetry. After all, poetry is a place where things can be (in a way) brought back to life.

I often think about a student I taught. He was in my 10th grade English class, until he purposefully drove off a cliff. I think about the windy road he took—how determined he must have been not to turn that wheel at the last minute. The toughest subjects to write about lend themselves to forms. For me, forms work like guardrails – they keep me on the road, even when I want to drive off of it. What I found "unsayable" took the form of a villanelle about being in the classroom just days after Victor was gone:

Villanelle for Victor

We studied Shakespeare, writing, parts of speech;
you sat in the first row across – three down...
the empty seat, and I'm supposed to teach?

You played in the school's band and loved the beach
last week, but now we're here and glances drown
your seat. *Grief* also is a part of speech.

15

So as a teacher, what is in my reach?
Is *this?* (I covered adjective and noun).
It's been three days, and I'm supposed to teach?

I don't want Desdemona to beseech
Othello for her life, and then his frown
as he ignores her desperate, pleading speech.

My students hold their breath, his hand, a leech,
arrests her life as she lies in her gown,
and this, today, is what I'm supposed to teach?

The clock hands tick, it's quiet now and each
of us remembers quiet as your crown.
We study Shakespeare, writing, parts of speech,
but I can't speak, and I'm supposed to teach.

The poem served as a way for me to contain the experience of my grief and put into words the impossibility I felt when trying to teach my class in the days after.

In poetry, I am always back in my circular childhood, but I am also simultaneously high above Long Beach, on that abandoned building— both tucked safely away and, at times, in danger. I am watching my favorite place in the world burn to the ground, but I am also still able to enter its cool hallways and smell its incense. Victor dies and dies and dies, but he also lives. I see him sitting at the desk in front of me. I hand him back his essay on *Othello,* and he smiles.

Part 1:
Field Trips

O, to take what we love inside,
to carry within us an orchard, to eat
not only the skin, but the shade...

— from "From Blossoms" by Li-Young Lee

Mummies of the World Exhibit
with My Young Children

Girls slink into dimming,
    enthralled by the play of light and cold

of each case, glass quiet and straight.
    How long is 1,000 years—

Sheath of material frayed and fringing
    on the edges, speaking in threads,

knees tucked, tether of bone and linen,
    our noninvasive looking.

For the forgetting
    there are signs: "These were humans."

What is a named thing here?
    What wrap makes arm into wing?

What happens to the brain? They ask
    if they can be made into mummies,

suggesting that if I were one
    I would be giving two thumbs up.

Do you close your eyes
    when you die? wonders the youngest

who says she hopes her own will
    stay wide open—

scrunches her forehead, amplifies
    their earthen-brown.

At home I need to run,
    pushing into pavement, flesh

vibrating on concrete and lung heave,
    my brain still shivering in its skull.

I imagine my calf muscles pulling away,
    undone from their sinews like rolls

of deli meat meant for slicing, like fabric
    unraveled for the cut.

Later, I pull covers tight around their chins,
    these girls, so light with life, even when eyes

are shut, quiet, preserved if for a moment,
    wrapped warm in the stillness of sheets.

Glitter Gulch

could be found in downtown Las Vegas
where her grandparents brought her to stay
at the Golden Nugget in the oven
of August. She didn't know what a *gulch*
was, but imagined it as green couch or disco—
swirled, dazzling, because of the light spilling
out of the double wood doors into the blinking
dark. Music squeezed through the crack,
pressed into her ears, cabs came down
Freemont street, topped with the girls' pictures,
fur and feathers, buzzing to pick up this person,
drop off that. The girls loomed, billboard
lips, candy-slicked. She kept wondering
about the gulch; clues told her it must
be something alive, fire consuming logs
or the singing upstairs at the old Italian restaurant,
Stefano's, where the waiters belted, *When the moon*
hits your eye like a big pizza pie. She didn't know
what *amore* was, but it must be like *gulch*,
wide but restrained, the world as unpeeled
orange, held just beyond her reach. She didn't
know yet that love and ravines had so much
in common, how impossible they were,
how quick each could become something else.

The Birth

No one warned how delicate you'd arrive,
how slow the oxygen would pull into lungs,
how your purple breath would loiter, then
splotch into complexion. Born then borne to
the clear, plastic cases warmed by sanguinity,
you settled into the machinery of saving: needle,
florescent bulb, bleach, monitor, protocol.

How many paintings have been made of hospitals,
or the doctor who plucks the baby like a dandelion,
hurries away from wind that will surely scatter her,
or the room where the newly alive try to breathe?
Better to capture the uncut field, the innocuous
picnic in the middle of summer, the ruddy mother
who opens a basket, the yellow flowers rooted

by paint. The kind of place where children laugh
like a creek, and there is never a chance of drowning—

Touring the B-17 Bomber at the Palm Springs Air Museum

(A Golden Shovel after Randall Jarrell)

They climb a slender ladder. From
stitched-together metal, my
daughters disappear into the plane, a mother's
intuition wanting them to sleep
longer in their not knowing. I
want to conceal how people fell
from the sky, how bombs glided into
their targets, how it happened in the
daylight, so everything hit. This *State*,

the state of being and of war. And
when they go further into the fortress, I
can no longer hear their hunched
tunneling. No oxygen masks needed in
this controlled air museum, its
planes are still. We are in the belly
of the third hanger, learning till
we are sick with statistics, my
eyes want to look away, wet
with sadness, with the soft fur
of faces that burned or froze.

My girls sit in the jump seats. Six
feet from ground, not miles
like the eight to ten men from
the past who flew this earth
in these planes, men loosed
into war, one man who crawled from
somewhere in this turret, from its
curved surface, with the dream
of getting home, with the want of
oxygen, and warmth and life,

someone's son, *someone's*, I
know this from Jarrell, how a man woke
into death. How am I to
explain these images of black
smoke trailing, or the definition of *flak*
or anti-anything? My girls and
their enthusiastic guide pause at the
plane's plexiglass womb, its nightmare
nested only the smallest fighters.

A single man curled knee to chin. When
my children emerge intact, I
hear the guide state how many died
but later, the girls tell me they
loved the plane, over washed
hair and brushed teeth, tell me
how some men were thrown out
because of their wounds, of
how their friends deployed the
parachutes, about the turret
and its smallness, tell me with
smiles, still unaware of what remains, a
poem, a person, a mess, a hose.

Huntington Beach Air Show

Punched up—the plane, pushed, rockets into sky,
engine rotating, coughs to catch on air.
The roar cuts off and sinks into a sigh
to mark the stall before the spiral stair
spin, wings careening down into the glisten
of salt, spectators stand and suck their breath
back in, no gravity, no noise. Listen
to the waves laugh until he makes the death-
defying turn, unfurling the metal straight
across the gleaming ocean like a sail
that's leapt right off the boat, its only fate
to fly. The crowd, still waiting to exhale,
yearns for relief, and on firm sand below,
a seagull, in disbelief, stares at the show.

Snorkeling

I did not follow you, masked, flippered,
wanting, into the mouth of the ocean, slippered
in darting eels, swathed in fish. I turned
to stay where sunlight murks, pools in the shallows,
where the water sits soft. You followed the sea's motion
to reef's sharpness, corals compressed with ocean.
So I did not witness when the gliding turtle broke
surface to sip air, as ocean slid and spoke
around you. As you floated—I had swum
to shore; you in paradise, I in panic.
You saw salt bloom where I saw skeletal death.
You heard the sea sighing. I heard jagged breath.

Le Corsaire

Organza flies against the threaded legs,
eight dancers wear the ocean in their clothes,
soft velvet blue of puffed up pants in pegs,
a swath of fabric twisted in the toes
of passion, music's fingers in her skin,
a shimmering tutu spins to catch the light,
and pirouettes propel her safely in
so he can gift her momentary flight.
We want the pirate leaping on the stage;
we want her moon-shaped foot, all leather bound,
the muscled thighs that beat like they have wings,
an orchestra to give our soundtrack sound.
Our bodies still, they sail to distant lands.
Applause leaves flesh and air between our hands.

He Refuses to Take Pictures in Pompeii

My husband puts his camera away.
The lens is best for light,
not the coarse ash rain burning down,
filling olive baskets,
sinking into cracks between cobblestones,
covering the bakery, the bodies of cats,
invading the lungs of old men and babies.
Bread is baking in brick ovens.
And then a moan.
An unintended scream.
A dog, twisting.
Earth sucked back her breath
and left the bones.
My husband does not want this recaptured in a photo.
He would like to be wearing black—
to have brought flowers.

Remembering You, Anthony Bourdain, at the Elementary School Talent Show

Most of these kids have yet to try sushi,
haven't left the country to taste the world,
still gravitate toward boxed macaroni
and cheese, but someday they might turn
on the TV to see you eat some strange food,
and witness the uneasy thrill of trying,
trying, trying something new.
This morning, at the elementary school,
an audience gathered between construction-
papered walls and a talent show began:
a boy played clear notes from a recorder,
a girl tap-danced across the carpeted floor,
someone sang, played the piano, delivered
a comedy skit full of terrible knock-knock
jokes followed by a drum's bada-ba,
then applause. You knew how to savor
an experience, how sitting with strangers
makes friends, that what we put in our mouths
matters—you pointed out the thread
spooled between us when we have a meal
together, the connection that takes place over
coffee or beer. This morning, after hearing
you were gone from this world, my daughter
danced on the stage, nervously taking a seat
at the table of the unknown. You would
have approved of these kids practicing
the art of taking risks. Someday
they might hear your voice and give up
using jarred garlic or eating in restaurants
on Mondays; or maybe they will recognize
that to taste is to experience, to try
means to live, or they will think back
to this elementary school talent show,
to this morning, where in the kindergarten

classroom, the chicks chirp under a warming
light. Where, just days ago, the children pressed
their faces to the glass as the eggs began to crack,
and from the shells emerged the broken,
scattered singing of new life.

Part 2:
These Children Frighten Me

All night your moth-breath
Flickers among the flat pink roses.

— from "Morning Song" by Sylvia Plath

September

The yoga instructor says,
tense your muscles tight,
so we clench inward, still
as stones mortared into walls,
then release. This gives us lightness
as we gather our mats, rolling
their patterns inward. Day-
to-day I use this to squeeze
fear farther into me,
so that like rocks metamorphosed,
it becomes something else:
the curved wave falling
into its crash, the small
shake in my mother's hand
when she holds her water glass,
the space of sky squeezed
enough to spark lightning,
even our own bodies
are a compression of the moment
where luck meets molecules.
I gather my daughter carefully
above school blacktop,
fold her in my arms,
press her tightly inward,
then let go.

Graveyard

When the cold of Fall sinks down into us,
you litter our lawn with plastic gravestones,

stony semblances, withered writing—
Beware. Spectacles to help us slice

through the world, where so many things
are casualties. Look, our little children

are lying among the markers, positioned
nicely, legs straight and still in the waving

grass. Listen, you can hear them breathe,
their small lives steaming from their mouths—

Fangs

She looked not-quite-right
at nine, wearing fangs—
I can only describe it as baffling,
her mouth botched with them,
her hair in tangles. The shoppers
stared. It was almost October 31st
in America. She slept with them half
in that night, swore they would keep
her safe. When they fell on the pillow
next to her, they seemed to glint
in the sharp moon-light—
little plastic knives.

On the First Full Moon Since I Was Attacked by a Werewolf

I relish in my new-found fur,
the way my teeth have needled, compact
muscles making my pajamas so tight
I changed into my husband's, and yes
I am worried the children, waking
to nightmares, will come down
to find me like this, and won't
recognize my soft howl at the dish moon,
or these hands, now paws, or claws,
that cannot type poems into a keyboard
or soothe them back to sleep, or even pour
a glass of milk. I have eaten a steak
from the freezer in three large bites,
but the cat has crept under the bed anyway,
so I sit awkwardly on the leather couch,
which I've probably ruined,
grinning, my new werewolf heart
pounding in the forest of my chest.

These Children Frighten Me

These children frighten me, their mouths, the ruin
of bones that sprout like rosebuds when they're teething,
their crescent-moon smiles bridge the afternoon,

the dark mush held in glass jars, pear and prune,
long wailing, paired with throated, labored breathing.
These children frighten me, their limbs, the ruin

of long nights without sleep, the blue raccoon
circles beneath eyes, my angry seething
crawls from its shell in the spoiled afternoon;

and sometimes things get thrown, a glare, a spoon,
a tantrum – we tiptoe around messes, weaving
between mislaid Legos, bruises, knees in ruin.

I have been told that all this ends too soon—
that I will often think back not believing
how small they were in Spring's coiled afternoon,

where seed sprouts, turns to blossom, sudden bloom,
and falls in sun, the necessary cleaving
that frightens me, the what if they...the ruin
of dawn to morning, of noon to afternoon.

Asbestos

Birthed out of fireproofing
on metal beams,
the word spins in the mouth,
cocoons in the lung's lining,
a slow, disastrous metamorphosis.

A variety of white moth
climbs out, undetected,
delicate, durable, impure,
it stretches
its mineral insidiousness—
an inhaled flapping of wings.

The unsettling is granularly soft:
the rattle of windows
or teeth in the bitter cold.

A Silver Reindeer in Southern California

is placed placid on the polish
of a wood piano.
It has spent eleven months
wrapped in a berry-red napkin
at the tinsel-filled bottom of a plastic bin
marked "Holiday," stuck in last year's
tree needles, between a glass menorah
and a cracked ornament.

It stands on leaden legs,
until one evening my daughter
gives him life, lifts him to fly through
flickering lights and cinnamoned air,
landing him so he can help pull
a sleigh through cotton-ball snow.

The next morning, she carries
him in her palm, leans him
over the rim of her half-eaten bowl
of frosted cereal, so he can drink
deep from the sweet, milky lake,
then lets him graze in the carpet yard
of Barbie's Malibu dream house.

That afternoon, she gallops
the reindeer over to visit
a gingerbread castle, peppermint
candied, dotted with jellies, constructed
near a pile of mandarin orange rinds
and a glossy beach shell.

She leans her ear near
his eyeless head, breathes in citrus
as she hears him sigh, sees the world
reflected in his shiny body.

On the Fourth Day of Hanukkah 2018

we watch Space X blast the Falcon 9 up
to the international space station carrying
smoked turkey breast, cranberry sauce,
40 mice and 36,000 worms for muscle
and aging studies. The rocket booster fires
against all that sky, a giant Menorah candle—
a miracle we can see against what we imagine,
like one day's oil turning into many.

I married into these traditions; my Latkes
are from Trader Joe's, I hum the Ma'oz Tzur,
not knowing the words, the song washing
around me, like the arms of two daughters
that wrap my waist, whose faces flicker
at night under the candles' glow. How they
ask me what will become of all those worms,
and I think *what will become of us all?*

By what miracles are we astonished? By birth,
death, resurrection, by oil that's lasted
and lasted, by a rocket carrying squirming
bodies and fruitcake. How different
our miracles are now—how the same—
how time is tied into itself, traditions
held onto like rescue ropes. How I celebrate
every miracle I can.

On the First Night of Passover

I sit next to a woman at dinner who makes sounds
for the zombies on *The Walking Dead.*

Magenta beet-horseradish stains our lips, drips
onto porcelain. My daughter smears the juice

across her plate and I think of the Hebrew parents,
how their hands must have trembled as they applied

the lamb's blood to their doorposts. How they must
have kissed their first-born sons before bed, how they

had to have thought, please let this work. We dip
fingers in the wine, press down once for each plague,

and say them all, as if saying them will keep them
on the page. When we are done, our dishes are dotted

with crimson, and I feel like making a zombie noise,
some guttural groan over the bitter herbs, dishes of tears,

shank bone, singing spun from our throats, haroset,
the crisp snap of matzo. *You know,* the woman whispers

over bites of brisket, *the zombies aren't the walking dead—*
and I know exactly what that makes us.

The Beach

A small girl is stung by a stingray's
flailing tail, and after she screams,
her mother carries her up, wrapped tight
in a yellow towel and waves down
the lifeguard from his tower.

While he pulls out the barb,
pours hydrogen peroxide over
the wound, bandages her foot,
my daughters are two buoys
tossed by hungry waves, blue

swimsuits fused with water, the rise
of their laughter lifting
in the air between us.
They do not hear the girl
crying over the soothing

growl of the ocean's mouth,
and I won't go to the shore
to tell them to listen.
Instead, they fling up their arms,
while the insistent sun presses

down on us all,
everything shimmering
sharp-tipped glass,
and the sky, cloudless and wide,
flaunts its emptiness.

Triangle of Life

We crouched beneath the desks during
earthquake drills. Remember when the thing
to do was hunker under all that splintered

wood, while we imagined the fitful jolting
of chalkboard, paper, asbestos-filled roof?
I followed the rules like bread crumbs...

My daughters inherit my safety; one wears
her helmet as she plays, *It's super safe*,
she says, looking both ways. The other

studies ballet, a form ripe with rules;
one, two, three; legs pinned by positions.
But hasn't the earth shifted?

Hasn't it changed? It's no longer
you and the desk, but a triangle
of space to stay in while learning is done

without a trace of chalk. Let the earth
quake! We know what to do! Or,
if we don't, we'll likely go on living

anyway. The three of us, taking shape,
shaking the old rules into the air
like confetti—

Part 3:
Ordinary Ends

Monsters are real, and ghosts are real too.
They live inside us, and sometimes, they win.

— Stephen King

Ordinary Ends

Mine is an ordinary life for sure—
most would concur.
Small sorrows, only ones that I can bear,
no rare disease, no sharp grief to endure
or not endure, no stifling lack of air

or freedom, no untethered need to drink,
no leaden breath,
no suicidal thoughts when by the sink
washing the dishes, no feet on the brink
of slipping to an early, soapy death.

Just small annoyances: knees that stay sore,
a twinging wrist,
remembering that I've read this book before
when half-way through, the never-ending chore
of crossing things out on my growing list

of things to do, small holes in well-worn clothes,
(I cannot sew)
a fierce desire to swim against the flow,
two willful kids, a husband that I chose—
all ordinary things, and yet I know

disaster sits, a winged thing waiting to
whir suddenly. I hear its patient sigh
in every ordinary moment. You
know, so do I—
that ordinary ends; all good things do.

To Robert Frost on a Frightening Evening

There are still woods, still soft swept snow,
Our leader's Tweets are scary though;
Enough so we can't keep our ear
Attuned to nature's splendid show.

What would you write if you were here?
You held America so dear,
Now fire and ice, such polar pairs
Seem tame to us compared to fear.

No laureate could climb the stairs
And help the swearing-in, no cares
To speak with sense, no way to steep
Our tea then turn to our affairs.

Our situation's dark and deep.
We have humanity to keep—
We're waking up and cannot sleep;
We're waking up and cannot sleep.

This Is an Alternative Poem

You can read it without
your eyes, without thinking.

That is not rain drumming
down on us, just buzzing
water bees in hollow ears.

It refuses to scream even when
you slide needles into its sides.

That is not a sky surrounding
us, that is just a cage of blue,
holding two halved animals together.

There is no paper to give it life.
Its grin is not a smile at all.

That is not the Earth, it is a rock
thrown haphazardly into the lake,
its wake traveling inward.

It is only letters, the likeness of words.
It won't ask *how do we do this?*

That is not America, stunning,
its glistening opportunities are
wet concrete tucked into crevices.

It will curl up quietly, shushing
itself. It has no punctuation.

That is not a woman holding
a sign. It is only an apparition
of cardboard and ink. A distraction.

You cannot read it. You are not listening.
Even now it is dry and drifting away.

The TSA Agent Knows

you paid good money for this.
You have been chosen
because your foot moved in the machine.
The scan lit up
your neck, chest, waist, arms, wrist, crotch.
The agent must feel with gloved fingers;
they cannot rescan you.
A private room is available
for your comfort.
This is for everyone's safety.
If you refuse,
they will escort you out.
They will put their hands in your pants waistband.
They will tell you what they are doing
before they do it.
Each place must be checked twice.
You will say thank you and sort of mean it.
Each place must be checked twice.
Before they do it,
they will tell you what they are doing.
They will put their hands in your pants waistband.
They will escort you out
if you refuse.
This is for everyone's safety.
For your comfort,
a private room is available.
They cannot rescan you.
The agent must feel, with gloved fingers,
your neck, chest, waist, arms, wrist, crotch.
The scan lit up
because your foot moved in the machine.
You have been chosen.
You paid good money for this.

Per Aspera Ad Astra

From Hardships to the Stars

It's 1977.
The US launches a time capsule
into space. The Voyager
Golden Records are constructed
of gold-plated copper,
coated in Uranium 238, so that aliens
can know its age.
The selection of the contents
takes a year.

The sounds:
surf, wind, thunder, whales,
hello in 55 languages, *Per aspera ad astra*
in Morse code, Bach
and Chuck Berry, brainwaves.

The images:
DNA, insects, Egypt,
Jupiter, humans drinking and licking,
a woman in a supermarket, a page
from a mathematics volume.

The instructions:
diagrams, time frames,
calibration tools, a pulsar map
of the solar system, the chemical
composition of the Earth's atmosphere.

We send this distillation
into interstellar space
with no guns, no images of war.

* * *

It's 1998.
Two astronauts hold
onto the international space station,
drops of humanity against its steel.

They cannot see
the woman being led away by her wrists.

They have shed the gravity of a man,
sitting on a curb, being read
his rights. They float
in a different darkness. Even though
they are tethered, their hands
grasp metal.

It's human nature
to hold on.

* * *

And now
everything is about containment,
but a new solar system is discovered.

They name its sun
Trappist-1 for the telescope
that can see it.

We imagine life on this rocky planet—
a chance of water,
a sky perpetually sunset salmon,
one side always facing the light,
an infant sun that will burn
for 10 trillion years.

What would we send
into space now?

Beliefs
are not easily unfastened—

even our voices
stick to our throats,

and we don't know
the consequences of letting go.

* * *

Jane Roe

(Norma McCorvey, Roe of landmark 'Roe V. Wade' ruling, passed away on February 18th 2017.)

The name conjures fish eggs
alchemied in the ovaries, life suspended.
You were impoverished, unwed, a freak show
barker turned side show, your womb,
a plum, swelling too quickly for the ruling
to do you any good. I can imagine
the underbelly of your grief. The frustration
of anonymity, of being so many things:
champion, nymph, Sisyphus, sub-sister.

Your life was simple, you said, all you wanted
was to empty the O of your womb, to "lay down"
you whispered, instead opening your body
to the world, so that Roe was only case
and not contents. Norma McCorvey,
your alibi was an 8th grade education, or eyes
that were only beginning to shutter open. Clawing
your way to the center of causes, you always ended
up in the margins, waiting to be born.

I wonder at your choice of baptism, if an ocean
would have been too wild, a church too still.
There is the smell of chlorine as he dips you in the pool,
your eyes closing tight, the dilation of your pupils,
undeceived? Death is not always the end.
We bury you as Jane and Norma.
The rhythm of your heart beating
back into the universe. The sun of our wombs
burning with you; the moon of our wombs weeping.

The Etymology of Silence

What it is not: the hum
of the refrigerator against the afternoon,
or the lap of the lake on the pebbled
shore, crickets in the evening.

Someone once gave me
a bottle of water for my sense
of humor. My quiet
is contagious – something
to be fought against,
to crack or cure.

This is why I go to the movies
with my friend
who laughs loudly over popcorn,
even at the previews—

imagine it on her breath,
like golden butter or tequila,
like a creek after a storm,
welled up, heaving, roaring into
its own steep banks.

Often, I wake up at 3:00 am,
from slouched sleep certain
I am dead.

Have you done this also?

It's late like this when
silence can't be pierced or prodded
or taken apart gently, but must be
broken suddenly, shattered
like crystal glass.

What it is: sleepers who swallow
their words in the condensed
darkness; and the reason the clock
has options for ocean waves, babbling
brook, and bird song—

My Daughters Will Never Know

the joys of home economics,
the room full of do-gooders, helpers,
sewers, piecing together pillow cases

and aprons; smiling with roses
in their cheeks, with soft hands
and sugared smiles. My daughters

will not be taught how to decorate
a table, will not suck in their bellies
with books on their heads, shoulders

pressed back with the possibilities
of marriage and musical notes spun
from kitchens. They will not learn

how to clean up after cooking
bacon, to pour a curling ribbon of soap
into the hot pan, to wet paper towels,

throw them steaming
into the sizzle of grease.
How will they survive?

Who will tell them how to avoid
the steely prick of needles?
How will they protect themselves

from the slick jaws of fabric shears?
Both are aware their limbs
belong to them, both know

they are their own canvas—
they cannot be adorned.
They are the flowers and the lace.

Acrylamide

A word you wouldn't know unless it was posted, eye-level, at every drive-through you visit. It's in the coffee, the bun, the fried potato, the cup, the wall. It crouches. They've even found it in prunes. There was a time you could enjoy a French fry without thinking about it; when you could bite into one and only contemplate the crunch of its salt, or the contrast of crisp outside and milky inside. Now I can eat only three before I start thinking about death. My mother-in-law orders her fries extra crispy. If they are not hot, she sends them back. I don't know if I should say anything. There is no regulation on how much we can consume. If there were, surely there would be a black-market for well-done fries. They give it to laboratory mice via drinking water. The mice get tumors. We get signs.

Grass

An unrulier word than *lawn*. The most natural substance on earth. Sugar cane is a sort of stiff, sweet grass that they can't grow in Hawaii any longer. Something about a rich guy not liking the smoke. You never hear anyone say *the grass always has more chlorophyll on the other side*. I have imagined it in museums someday. The docent says *this is grass. If you were lucky, you'd have had it in front of your home. If you were really lucky, you'd have had it behind your home also.* The children run up to run their hands through it. Gap had a fragrance named *Grass*. They discontinued it though. If you want to buy it, it will cost you over $100 an ounce. If you were drawing grass, and had a Crayola box, you might use *Inchworm, Asparagus* or *Forest*. None of them would look right. None of them would contain any chlorophyll at all.

Part 4:
Where Life Has Been

Then leaf subsides to leaf.
So Eden sank to grief,
So dawn goes down to day.
Nothing gold can stay.

— from "Nothing Gold Can Stay" by Robert Frost

Votive

You always pulled me with you
like a living shadow. The church
floorboards sung

out against our feet. Stained glass
drew blue morning light into Santa Ana's
Church of the Messiah,

where a square wooden table sat heavy
with glass candles. Some of them burned.
Others stood,

full with wax and waiting. I remember
you dragging match against box strip,
the concentrated chemicals flowering

into life at your fingers.

After reading *The Dollhouse Murders*

I ask my parents take the dollhouse
and store it in the garage. In the book,
the dolls come to life, and the little girl wakes
each morning to the smallest figurines,
two inches of terror, in different rooms
than where she left them. One doll closes
the curtain of the imaginary window,
another poses, hand over stifled mouth,
sits on the couch, stares into air.

I couldn't close my eyes at night, knowing
they didn't, not even if they wanted to.
There was always a door, slightly open,
or a mark on the flowered wallpaper
that hadn't been there before.
Even after I covered the house with a quilt,
and slept with the lights on, I could still hear
the brittle scratches of doll plastic and wood,
the baby crying from the yellow crib.

Reading brought those dolls to life: they
breathed and sighed and had to be laid
into shoeboxes. That was the beginning.
Soon, there were siblings locked in our attic,
then a mad woman. Every dog had rabies,
each storm drain contained a clown. Books
hook their fingers into our eyes. We can't
help but open their covers, unshuttering
the crisp, white page—the indelible, dark ink.

The Two Indians I Knew
(from *Indian in the Cupboard* and *Little House on the Prairie*)

were flat ink pressed in pages that breathed
on my white, wood childhood bookshelf.
One was plastic, animate only when taken
out of his cupboard; his tomahawk sharp, but trivial.
He only sought the simplest things—food, a teepee, fire
to sit by and think, and because a story-bound boy found
him alive, he gifted the Indian everything, but in miniature.

The other, penned on a prairie, intruded into the log
cabin in the woods to smoke Pa's tobacco and scare
Ma, who tried to hide the baby and kept frightened eyes
until he gave a gift (with feathers!) to Laura and left. Leaving
a trail of hoof-prints on tall grass—the small thunder
of freedom, followed by a *whoop*! or some other
joyful noise to put everyone at ease.

How easy to think of Helvetica Indians then, shut out
of a log cabin, or into a cupboard for safe-keeping.
Drums, face paint, a deep grunted: *How.* A slick
brown horse. Energetic enough to gallop, whinny, run
miles into the horizon and dissolve over the edge
of the earth. At night, I could close the books' covers
on it all and sleep a child's sleep.

Now, the once one-dimensional words blur
into something bitter. I do not know whether
to shelve them or give them to my children,
prompt them to open the waxy paper, to coax
out what is hidden, how to teach *stereotype*
as I tuck them into their blankets, promising
better books in the quiet dark of a new night.

Bertha

Ay, dead as the stones on which her brains and blood were scattered.

What did the teacher think when I wrote this
as my favorite line in my sixth-grade *Jane Eyre*

book report? The image, plastered in my head,
red and rock, the lingering remains of you.

What did I know of attics or governesses?
And all I knew of stones is what it felt like to skin

my knees. Anything would have looked beautiful
against their inflexibility, the bright softness of life

pooling on them. Bertha, we all have our attics
with fascinations tucked away inside, parts

of our former selves waiting to emerge—
I did know something of madness, of black hair

that made me see myself in you. I also knew
something of escape, of climbing over the security

fence of the ten-story building on my childhood
block, of laboring up the fire stairs to the tennis courts

on top. I'd sit on the ledge for hours breathing
in bus smog, always aware there could be no story

without you, who set the house in flames then leapt,
who reddened the stones until it was all I could see.

Most of us hold on to our coursing blood, we turn
day after day to find out what will happen next—

I always climbed back down, lucky enough to have
a way, part of me held captive on that page.

What I Really, Really Want

Give me a skating rink,
eight neon-green wheels, a disco floor
where it's 90's night, every night.
Give me a flannel shirt, a pair
of Guess jeans. Give me Kurt Cobain.
Give me his cheerleaders,
the ones that jumped
just the way we felt, like we were full-
of-life zombies. Give me a tin
of Maxwell House instant vanilla latte,
that lived in the cupboard before Starbucks.
Give me a good game of Oregon Trail.
Give me dysentery and four oxen.
Let me leave in March so I can avoid
the worst part of winter. Give me two
hours at a park where everyone hears
the grass. Give me French fries without
acrylamide, a Bob's Big Boy, an Arnold's
Family Restaurant. Give me a phone
with a rubbery, spiral cord and plastic,
square buttons. Let me push each
button hard, hear every clear, single tone,
call a yellow cab an hour before
we need it. Give me Steve Urkel,
or at least a set of leather bound
Encyclopedias, where I can look
things up alphabetically, where Alexa
can't say, *I don't know the answer
to that*. Give me a television show
with a woman whose bangs defy gravity,
give me the time during the commercials.
Give me an episode of *Girls Gone
Wild* at 10 pm, and Lorena Bobbitt
on News at 11. Give me a VHS player,
rewind button, let me hear the whirl
of tape going backward so I can walk

across the street to Blockbuster and drop
it in the slot before midnight.
Give me the song "1999" before 1999,
before Y2K, when everybody thought
the world was going to end;
when the world, as we knew it, did—

Fillet

My mother makes dinner
almost every night:
white china plates, checked cloth napkins,
glasses of whole milk.

This night there is a steak centered
on each plate—
Porterhouse; half strip and half fillet.
I eat

the strip first, in small bites between
salad, pushing
the fillet to the side of the plate for last.
My father must

have still been in his suit.
I remember
the starched straight collar and how
I blinked

as he reached across the table's wood,
stabbing
my fillet with the four prongs of fork,
half-smiling,

placing the piece in his mouth, saying
Yum
between rows of white teeth. Telling me,
you should never

save the best for last—it might not be there
when you are ready for it.

Prince Working

He rides traffic, embraces numbers,
keeps a starched collar and pants
with pleats,

fashions grim reports for clients,
swallows briny martinis, French kisses coffee,
eats

air conditioning and florescent lights,
defends the office, dismisses his break,
beats

the clock with glossy eyes,
is paid in automatic deposits
for his feats.

Work

1. The Fast Food Restaurant
That work that gets inside and never leaves,
like French fry fat and golden arches arched
above the building, etched in thread on sleeves,
while through the tired hours burgers marched
in bags and boxes, filled the room with grease
that couldn't be scrubbed off, her fingers slick
with food that wouldn't rot, each bun, each piece
of nugget not quite chicken, but a trick
done quick with breading, covering up grey-
gristled *stuff*, what else could it be named?
The sizzled smell, the red burn that would stay
on skin, its tender territory claimed
with basket crisscrossed branding that would lurk
across her arm, a symbol of this work.

2. The Bank
Across her arm, a symbol of this work,
a starched shirt sleeve for air conditioned rooms,
hot-coffee flooded mornings in berserk-
horned traffic, red lights blink, the vacuum zooms
on early morning carpet in the bank
before the customers arrive, she sits
uncertain what to do, the chilly yank
of thin papers from thick piles, at her wits
end, the only chatter the keyboard's keys,
and clicking high-heels across a glossy floor,
she thinks *at least its temporary – please
let summer go by fast, let there be more—*
than secretaries, desked, with skirted hips,
another coat of lipstick on their lips.

3. The Statistics Department
Another coat of lipstick on her lips,
her boss is French, and always wears black pants,
and drinks hot tea, in small sufficient sips,

goes off on walks, sometimes goes off on rants
about the university. The girl
leaves early from work almost every day
after filing applications in the curl
of manila folders, studies, gets her pay,
listens to her French boss telling her how
she won't work on her birthday, but instead
she'll pop champagne in the shower, vow
to live, then pour the bubbles on her head—
this is the best job that she's ever had...
she lives a little sweeter, a little sad.

4. The Candy Shop
She lives a little sweeter, a little sad,
works at the shop on Santa Barbara's pier
where a threadbare turkey pecks away like mad
at salt-water taffy, where lemonade flies leer
and dive right in, their sugary deaths in vain,
scooped out with plastic spoons, secretly, trashed,
buried beneath boxes, their contents lain
in the long, back-lit, glass case, where she's stashed
the chocolates, sour ribbons bright with fruit,
square-wrapped caramels, gummy bears, and ropes
of licorice, toffee peanuts warmed, her loot
waiting in white bags, folded over with hopes
for jobs that pay more than minimum wage
and candy, she gets her BA, turns the page.

5. The PR Firm
Her BA's on the wall, she turns the page
of the press release, scans the text for errors,
another office, air-conditioned cage,
crammed with phone calls, bankers, lawyers, bearers
of bad news, long lunches, suits, and happy hours
that aren't so happy, filled with handshakes, hectic,
turn to dark dawn, even the coffee cowers
in its pot, awaiting the eclectic
mouths that will consume it, gulp by gulp;
she's trapped inside a Fourdrinier machine,
pulverized then pressed into a pulp,

refined and bleached to bone-white, thin, routine,
typed and proofread, indelible ink
on so many things: the task, the call, the brink—

6. The Public School Classroom
On so many things: the task, the call, the brink
of something new, she's hired in a pinch
to teach kids how to read and how to think
about their reading, slowly, inch by inch
she fills the room with books, she's twenty-two
now, this used to be a science-class
room, and now she's tasked with breaking through
the webs, the dirt-crawled classroom, taking glass
jars off the shelves, what's in them looks like brains,
or something worse, the students take their seats,
they read, she learns the unexpected pains
of calling child protective services, meets
the officer, in charge, who doesn't know
if the girl will be alright or where she'll go.

7. The Home
That work is done for now so where she'll go
can't be known, she watches her belly grow,
her ankles swell, veins river small and blue,
the girl births girls and all work becomes new
and strange, the work of keeping things alive,
by spoonfuls, fears that suddenly arrive
like swarms of bees, like locusts in a field
of blooming flowers, the work of orange rinds peeled
back, of apples sliced, of kissing knees,
of teaching *right* the work of teaching *please*,
the work of letting go, the work of loss
that travels through the body, weaves across
the workings of the heart, the way it cleaves—
that work that gets inside and never leaves.

Ong Namo

Opening my eyes
or lowering anything will break
the meditation, my head light
will snuff out, the hovering ego
bullying its way back into my chest.

She keeps telling us to *breathe in.*
Breathe in. Now *breathe in* some more,
and when we are about to pop,
she says, *just a little more,*
but I'm letting small, secret breaths slip out,
and that is probably why my day will be
no good.

If only I were doing this right—
focus, breathe, root—hold
the air in my chest more tightly, my lungs
would likely collapse, but the day would glow,
bright with hungry Kundalini fire dragons,
howling, releasing their sharp-edged energy,
galloping into life.

The dust of incense falls
to the floor.
I roll the mat
slowly. The flowers fold
into each other and disappear.

Miss Bonner

Miss Bonner turns away from us,
her eyes close, her blonde becomes a curtain.
We lean forward from the floor,
legs criss-crossed and wonder-eyed.

She raps three times, deliberately
on the worn wood-backed rolling chair.
Her audience is more and more still, quieter
with each thump; we can hear the breath

of whoever is next to us, the comforting
rustle of her long skirt as she turns back
around. We know she will be transformed.
There is magic in her chair, in her hand

that knocks a new personality into her body.
One day she is an old woman, with voice
folded over at the edges, with slow hands,
her invisible cane in arthritic fingers,

her glistening eyes get wider and wiser.
Another day she is seven, just like us, bright-
cheeked and boisterous, jumping breathless
into the classroom air, clapping.

Later, she will be a long-legged pirate, pursuing
all the treasures of the world, enraptured,
clutching some hand-drawn, weather-edged map.
We won't ask where she got it, why she travels,

in these ten minutes a day, how her body
becomes so many, arriving like rainbows or recess.
She must still be there with us while we make
coffees, assemble lunches, wonder *what happened?*

Today I sit at the dining table, my hand curled
into itself. I find the wood three times. Worry flies
from fingers. The old woman winks, the seven-year-old
giggles, the pirate raises his sword into the sparkling sun—

It Was Already the Beginning of the End

I'm your biggest fan.

—Annie Wilkes in Stephen King's *Misery*

In a garage in Isla Vista, you asked if I wanted
to see your Stephen King collection, and being
an ingénue and at my very first frat party,
I climbed the beer-stained stairs to a room
that held a bookcase—with books!

Next to Economics 101, Astronomy, Calculus,
I found *It, Dolores Claiborne, Gerald's Game,
The Stand* – I could go on, but the point
is there was enough there to know
you were someone I could spend
the rest of my life with.

King is part of our lineage, this fact
would set us up for an avocado tree
that refused to grow fruit, the cat that sunk
its teeth into our arms, the blood
of babies, birthday cake, the shift-shaping
of our own faces, teeth extractions, over-done
dinners, lost scissors, front row seats
for watching parents disappear
into their skin.

Even now, in the quiet living
room, I hear the tick of the wind
in the fig branches or the clawing
of winter leaves against the street and know
it's inevitable.

Two of us will become one
and then none, and those books
were simply a foreshadowing
of every hungry lake that will eventually drown us,
every unwashed knife, every dressing and un-
dressing, the fact that we will
suffocate or starve.

I am okay with it.

Here's to heavy breaths,
a backward glance, the wrinkle
deepening across my forehead—

"I'm Not Afraid of Death; I Just Don't Want to Be There When it Happens."
—Woody Allen

He loves to watch those scientific shows:
the sun burns down, sea turtles sweep the sand
to make it to the ocean from the land.
He's worried, speaks in several quiet *no's*
because the newly born are in the throes
of seagull beaks, all picked apart and fanned
until their remnant shells litter the strand
of beach with death, and so I think, *he knows
too much of this by now.* He turns to say
that only five percent of them will live—
he's cheering for the five inside his head,
Come on sea turtles! Willing life to stay,
alive when so much is already said
and gone. He leaves the room to mourn the dead.

Orchids

When they are mostly dead,
your friends bring them to you. Veined
and spotted open-mouthed soldiers
standing bloodless on the counter.

Nothing rivers through the stems.
They cannot even slouch.
You replant them, tuck their roots,
add bark and moss, cut

stems, mend the wounds
with cinnamon. Early mornings,
when the sun spills across the kitchen,
the newest orchids are born back

to life. They stare at you with their sepals,
send tubers out, green and full.
This morning, one licks its yellow
labellum and smiles. It's hard to tell

who is growling, who is yawning.
Something so aware requires a strange
discipline. At times, you want to let
the petals turn thin. You wish they would

give up their green. Instead they follow
orders. When your friends come over,
they ask which is theirs. You don't keep
track. They run their eyes up and down

each sticky stem like they regret
what they have done. When they leave,
the orchids sneer, then go back to pressing
their faces to the window's winter sun.

Sticks

for Bob Ross (1942-1995)

On a wet canvas anything is possible, color
is stretched, added; all of a sudden, the sky
becomes Phthalo Blue, it just happens.
He pulls paint for the perfect shade of sunset—
bet you didn't realize you had so much power,
he says. My daughter straightens her shoulders
as he pushes the mountain down into the mist
and washes the brush, *no pressure, it's up to you.*
The only pressure applied is to the brush:
beat the devil out of it. He thwacks
the bristles on the side of the easel
until the brush is clean.

This is his plan for painting mountains.
My daughter follows the fan brush;
its sweep bends the light, slips
down the mountain's sides until an avalanche
of texture appears out of the air. *Titanium
White*—his voice slides into our home.
He says *light,* and its color sticks to the canvas.
My daughter concentrates on the brightness—
a little snow, a happy little cloud. He strokes a valley
into existence. *Imagine all the things
that can live there.*

Here, the world is whatever we want it to be.
He scrapes another peak into the side,
slices the pink sky with darkness, brings
the green half-way up the slope. *It gets too high,
the trees can't live where it's so cold.* He mixes
the black and the blue—a bruise
on the palette—shadows the left sides where the light
doesn't hit. He finishes a tree branch, scatters
a few Dark Sienna sticks into the ground
to show where life has been.

Part 5:
Disassembling

The dark ending does not cancel out
the brightness of the middle.

— from "I Have Good News" by Tony Hoagland

My Mother Takes the Axe

My mother takes the axe and swings an arch—
it whooshes through the air, hits wood on sand,
the night is coming with its silent march,
and wood for kindling must be chopped by hand.

Us three kids watch her gracefulness until
the axe blade seems to slice down with the sun
and catches finger-tip and then she's still
for just a moment, and what's done is done.

She asks for ice and reaching to the ground,
she picks her finger up, says she's alright,
instructs us she'll *be back, don't make a sound,*
and drives herself away into the night.

The tip was trashed, she said, us three kids trembling
at the prospect of our mother's disassembling.

Parts of My Mother

My mother's hands at 10 and 2,
driving, roasting chicken, setting

a table, folding her fingers into straight
cloth napkins. My mother pumping

gas, leaving her eyes on the man
in the low-rider next to us, insisting

he turn down his music, her voice hooks
into his skin. My mother writing her heart

into letters to the editor about trash
choking up the riverbed or cars

making deliveries from middle lanes—
so illegal... how could they? My mother

laughing her head off at lunch, cracking
up over the classical music, at the waiter

serving coffee in the slanted sunlight,
who whines *cofffeeeee?* ... drawn

out and nasally, like he's better
than everything, but the steam still

leaks out of his silver coffee pot,
like my mother's ha ha's; she

is snorting. What else is there to do
in life, when confronted with yourself,

but laugh? Later, my mother remembers,
serves us streams of milk in delicate

porcelain cups. She hoots, tearing up,
unable to hold herself together—

Bell's Palsy

The flecks of panic swim inside your eyes
when drooping started slowly at your lip.
Mystified, your mouth, an anchor, tries
to hold each bite, to apprehend each sip.
The shell of bony ear canal turned noun,
no longer verb, eye stuck and gawking out,
a patch to press it, faulty cheek draped down,
its tissues in an adamant reroute.
So movement becomes theory now, refurled,
since brain and face do not connect, but slink
away, as if, belonging to the world,
they say when what is human cannot blink.
Each body finished even as we start,
pressed close a moment, then blown wide apart—

The Eye

The ophthalmologist points out the optic nerve,
where eye signals the brain to make contours,

lights, darks. My eye has become a specimen.
I remember scraping the connective tissue

from a cow's eye ball in Biology class, the rubbery
remnant protruding from the back, the cornea

round, black and milky, like a rotten olive.
I felt horrible for the cow, for its empty

eye socket, its reduction to iris, vitreous humor,
pupil, lens. Our teacher insisted

we pluck each piece gently out, say its name,
pen a label on the diagram next to the scalpel.

Now I see life through that eye, remembering
its essential roundness, its elastic tendon,

my own body closer and closer to some science
experiment I can't yet put a name to.

Things

She slipped the glass into her purse, the drinks
are so expensive here—they'll never mind...
she mouthed the slice of orange down to the rind;
the thirties never left her, so she thought,
hold on to what you can. Her thin arm fought
to find mine until we were intertwined—
she never did like leaving things behind.

It's been thirty years since then, the memory clinks,
a Cheers! to savored guilt, a small reprieve
from all the stuff she's giving me that I
don't want to take. The sun folds in the sky,
as she finds those items that she's loath to leave:
that Vegas glass; a softly wilting blouse.
I take the things—twilight takes the house.

Echo

The morning I go to say goodbye, the sunrise
gnaws the horizon, spills its flesh over

the hot September sky, sucks moisture from
your mouth, so it hangs dry as city dust.

When I was small, I'd watch you work, your voice
swimming like a magnificent silver swordfish

across the construction yard. You held me with hands
thick from mixing concrete for swimming pools,

with sun-warmed arms solid from building.
This morning, your body seeps like a fumarole field,

weeps its energy into the world like a parent pours milk
into cereal bowls, like I pour bravery

into my legs so they will walk into the room.
Even my feet whimper, your breaths are rocks

in my shoes. If I could shake them out, I'd throw
them into the sun, watch them burn back to life.

Your surrender is a shudder, not the storm
I imagined, but rain leaking through windows.

I had never tried to hold an echo. I couldn't know
how it would feel in my hands. The blisters

it would leave. How it would fall through
my fingers and I would keep grasping.

To My Grandma, Who Always Liked to Play Pretend and Who Would Give Us Bells to Ring When We Were Sick

I was eleven when we took the elevator up
with the maid to the top floor of the Las Vegas
Hilton where we weren't allowed, and followed
her down the hall in the noontime, doors cracked
for cleaning, and we walked into one, like we

belonged. The suite had a glossy baby grand,
a room that later we'd see in a Demi Moore
movie and our breath would catch,
remembering how your eyes stayed on each item,
how you'd always buy vintage, strip it down,

re-staining until it glowed, pile extra throw
pillows on all the couches, flock a pink tree
at Christmas, drape cotton-ball snow across
the credenza, walk through the halls
Nivea lotioned, spritzed with perfume.

We'd dress up in your closet, metal heels, flowing
garments with built in bras, stirred water cocktails
behind the bar, ice clinking against old fashioned
glasses. While you meringued lemon pies, we played
grown-up, threw our heads back, drug

the bottoms of those gowns against green shag
carpet, hung onto banisters, swam circles
in a cornflower pool. Now, I am pretending
you are here, your hand on my shoulder,
your voice, every bell, ringing—

I Can Almost Picture You Standing
Over My Grave

because even though I am forty and you are only nine,
I hope I'll know you at any age;

because when my father-in-law died, my mother-in-law bought
additional single plots;

because when we go there to visit, we carry garden rocks
to station on his headstone;

because your father will be left of me and a stranger named
Bruce will lay just to my right;

because the lawn mower does not turn easily and has scratched
gray lines in the black granite;

because you will only get more freckled, but your eyes will stay
the shade of autumn grasses;

because the San Fernando Valley sun is unrelenting—
your cheeks will pink with it;

because on special days they serve free hot dogs, and you'll have one
banded with bright, red ketchup;

because you will go there—twice a month, then twice
a year, and then when you can,

because I've seen you pour water on the stone, and lovingly,
with quiet hands, wipe it clean.

Edges

The blades burn through the dewy graveyard green,
she grasps the trimmer, pushes between graves
and sometimes says out loud the names she saves,
the dates she cleans, so that they can be seen.
Can she do that? This cemetery queen
who reigns, her glinting trimmer-scepter waves
with pleasure, cutting verve to shreds, she paves
the way as verdancy flings from machine,
like waving arms that try to gather back
all that they've lost, all that's been tucked away,
all that's below, all that has taken flight.
The fresh-cut smell goes skyward with each hack;
she slices grass to gone perhaps to say
when people ask her, that she is alright.

2:00 AM

Our ancestors used sand

        or shadows, or swinging pendulums,
     anything that could be counted on
  to keep the days,
intervals, bienniums, eras—

    our way of gathering the universe,
      packaging it gently into
        nanoseconds, ages, epochs.
          The clock replaces the bell

      as a mathematical tool.
    We manipulate the time
  to play golf after work,
or drive in the waning daylight

  to the Spring baseball game.
    I miss turning back a clock,
      gently moving the arms
        through the hour.

    Now I only change
  the time on the microwave,
and the electronic gods take care
of everything else.

The Window

When I come home to it shattered,
at first it looks as if the glass
has had too much of itself, cracked

to a web, refusing to fall to the ground,
but each piece clinging
to the other, a mosaic already made—

One doesn't know what one will come
home to. In the afternoon, my husband
arrives, having fallen

from his bike after the rain's masked
the road with moss. His elbow, scraped
along the asphalt, bleeds. He squeezes

Neosporin—a pea, pulls the thin, waxy
covers off a bandage, performs the acts
that make us feel un-cut. I have never been

a good nurse. He does this all before
the fractured window—but that is a window,
and this is my husband, so I try:

cook buttered rice, simmer a soup,
pour water into clean glasses filled with ice,
the ways I know how to soothe. Steam

climbs from the pot as his arm begins
to bruise. The window has no such
inclinations. It still fogs, still shows

the cypress, refracted, through
the rutted glass. A bird still flies across
what looks like the entire broken sky.

Exhaust

My mom won't take baths
when my dad is home. It's too risky:
the lavender bubbles, glass
of champagne, imagined footsteps
up the carpeted stairs, the door cracking
open, the hairdryer, which happens to be
sitting on the tile, plugged-in, slips
from his hands into the bath. The obituary...
an unfortunate accident—No one
would figure it after forty-nine years
of marriage, there would be no questions.
They've been this way for decades.

Me, a kid, only started to understand
when I saw *Sleeping with the Enemy*
for the first time. You know the one—
where Julia Roberts comes home
to perfectly lined-up bath towels,
cans stacked flawlessly in the kitchen.
When I visit other cities, when I happen
into a one-bedroom apartment, sparse
yet warm, with historic flourishes, a few
coffee cups in the cupboard, I think,
*This is where I would like to live if
something happened to you.*

Once, at the market, after we disagreed
on creamer and lunch meat, after I complained
of the heat and you shivered in the vegetable
section, after we carried the honey-crisp
apples in one of our reusable plastic bags,
as I loaded those bags into the trunk,
you had already climbed in, started
the engine; and I breathed in the car's fumes,
sure you were going to back over me.

Blame it on my parents.
Blame it on that movie, those perfect towels.
Blame it on the exhaust. Yes, the exhaust—

The House

Around the edges of the yard are plants, tangerines
with their nostalgic seeds, sweet limes, bushes of rosemary,

hot peppers, everything rustling, flying, a jumping
spider crawls with its tiny fangs down the side of stucco,

a lizard keeps watch on sun-soaked concrete. Sometimes
we twist grapefruits off their branches to eat in sections,

the pink flesh sweet-sour, citrus dust on our fingers.
Often things feel so beautifully strange that I expect to turn

the corner and find a door to Narnia, a secret garden, a portal
that will transport us all to another dimension. We try

to tame everything, cut back the plants, cup bugs back
outside, sweep airplane dust from all the corners. One day

we come home to bee bodies, curled commas littering floors,
unsure as to how they found their way in. Here I am, halfway

through my life, so many things still eluding me. Small
mysteries. The snail's slow approach to the patio, its alien

antennae, its inscrutable skin. The way the sky darkens
and flowers fuchsia all at once, how my eyes keep changing

in the house's mirrors. How I already hardly recognize
myself. The house has become a living thing and we,

for now, its chambered heart, its rooms full
of breathing, its hallways like ventricles.

Chicken

Unwrapping you from your reasonable
packaging, I always feel some remorse

and carry your body tenderly to the pot
to lay you on your bed of citrus and sliced

onions, and pepper your skin with salt.
One time, I reached inside you to find

a neck and two hearts, unsure if any
were yours. There are over nine billion

of you alive, and still, each time I hold
you almost whole like this, slumped

and singular, like a small, cold baby,
your body goose-pimpled and clean,

I imagine your short, sharp journey
to here, seven weeks to market weight,

the assembly-line suspension
by two feet and low lighting, the stun

of electricity or carbon-dioxide,
a rub-bar on your breast, a single cut

to the throat, evisceration, chilling,
giblets sorted, your body

bagged. I heat you past your original
temperature to 165 degrees Fahrenheit,

until joints loosen, and bones turn
velvet. And after I have swallowed you,

in the dish-filled evening kitchen, I find
I am alone.

Part 6:
Eyes

and the pond was—I could see as I laid
the last peach in the water—full of fish and eyes.

— from "The Leaving" by Brigit Pegeen Kelly

The Cow

When I was a child we traveled on a plane
to Ontario, Canada to visit the family

I saw periodically. We took a day trip
to a place with cows and carried with us a loaf

of bread to feed them. One of the cows opened
her mouth, stuck out a tongue splotched pink

and black, as wide as a dinner dish, teeth
as big as dominos. The piece of bread sat soft

in my palm, which shook a little as I plopped
it down on the tongue and it vanished, like that—

disappeared first into the cow's dark throat,
then into one of the four stomach chambers

we had read about. I only knew small bites
into a square slice, and so it seemed miraculous

when the cow swallowed—and the bread
was gone. Later, the horizon swallowed

the sun, the night swallowed us into its darkness,
the aunts and uncles swallowed me

into their strange arms, the plane's thin
metal swallowed us back to Long Beach,

on the opposite coast, where lying in bed,
I thought of the magic that one cow

had accomplished and felt the loss
of everything irretrievable.

Corn

Once when I was five she offered
her teeth to me, her smile

a salmon, her bread-soft hands pointing,
laughing at the emptiness of a mouth,

then slid them back, delighted.
This is not her homeland. Her language

can't tell me the story of the teeth
or give them to me, can't pour grains

of them, like rice, shattering into a pot.
Those done bones, where did they go?

Now we walk in the whisper of corn
rowed in her back yard. She cradles

its fruit then yanks, quick, from the stalk,
peels the husk to small, compact kernels.

This is what she offers, not the wisdom
of words, but the care of growing

something that can nourish. Some thing
that starts underneath and rises,

blossoms, carries its seeds, is created
to be consumed. The sun slices through

those desiccated stalks, the sweet milk
strains underneath.

Blackberries at Six

I picked blackberries off bushes
with eager hands, horded them into me
as if they were gold or wishes, draped
across the still-green branches
of early Fall. I shoved them into my mouth
until everything turned bruise-purple:
until my fingers and lips turned,
until my teeth turned and the tip of my nose
and even my stomach
must have looked like a plum, swollen
with those small-beads. Even the sky
flushed florid, royal between stretched-
out clouds. In that dark thicket, the bitter
sweetness of sunset not yet on my tongue—
I hadn't found a sour one.

The Yellow Watermelon

Your gasp cut through
kitchen summer air
as I pushed the knife blade

through the other side:
green-striped skin to green-
striped skin, the halves

pulling away, the ruptured
split to the unexpected—
you had only seen glossy

pink-red insides over
and over. Imagine waking
to a magenta sky or the grass

suddenly blue, the world
turned sideways. Your surprise
when the flesh presented itself

marigold, as if the sun itself
was buried in those emerald
walls, waiting for escape.

Will it taste the same?
Your mouth found flesh, bit
into delight condensed

in impossible fruit. The world
holding itself out to us, slice
after astonishing slice—

The Lime

(A Triple Tritina)

Sylvia points to the tree, asks for a lime
for fish. Yellow fissures between the clouds—
the neighborhood is suddenly raining sun.

I twist a toad-colored fruit. Sylvia's son
is in her yard, closing boxes with lime-
green masking tape. A shiver clouds

her thoughts. She'd like to fly like the clouds,
run in her maroon sweatsuit to her son,
feed him from her breast again. The lime

of the lime, the clouds in her eyes, receding sun.

She doesn't want my help. Her cane taps
from the tremble of her sun-flecked hand;
I carry the lime, set it on her window

sill, so she won't have to bend. This window
is where she fed her husband soup, while "Taps"
played in his head in twenty-four notes. Her hand

was steady then, her son was young, his hand
dug for dinosaur bones in the dirt by the window.
Clouds clot, rain arrives and taps

the lime, taps the hand-taped boxes, the window.

The cracked sidewalk turns from silver to slate.
This is Sylvia's 2,000[th] rain in this house.
The son holds a broom like a weapon, sweeps

the worms from the walk. The rain sweeps
the artwork lined in chalk from the slate-
slabbed driveway of a neighbor's house.

I wonder what the cardboard boxes house;
if they can stand the rain. My gaze sweeps
their outer shells, the layers soaked, it's late.

It's late. In the house's window, the lime weeps—

Peach Stones

*(for Mount Calvary Monastery, which burned to the ground on
November 14, 2008)*

Mount Calvary Monastery chants
its matins—the voices, guttural liturgy
formed from lungs, lives, and listening.
The service sung in bits of sun,
no stained glass here, just wood beams
wooden seats, wishes, winged-things
flitting in the garden, sun climbing
from its salty cradle into the metal
scaffold of the monastery cross,
bronze and old, like silence and tea
swept through the spidered halls,
heavy voices floating, finding refuge
relief, relics, rendering a rest spot
for peace for place for peeling
the sun's skin back behind the mountain
until its blood grew, flew from hands
from garden to garden—a fiery bird
moving fast and holding fast,
finishing each floorboard,
each ceiling beam, book, and bench,
billowing its incense, birthing
singeing into singing through
ashes and dust, the empty archway,
the bell, a painting, a telescope, a cello,
the astonishing cross and the chanting,
voices like peach stones
divested of their flesh—

Hymn

This morning I walked the hall
to birdsong, not the normal
chatter, but full-fledged singing,
a choir of them perched between
fig-tree branches, warbling,
sun-soaked, the song falling
into my ears, *I didn't even ask
for this*, I thought, where
had I heard such agile notes
before? And then my mind went
momentarily to the monastery,
burned down eleven years ago,
where, grandmother, you drove us,
winding up the road higher
and higher until we opened
the car doors to the same music.

I can't help but think some birds
in this tree must be descendants
of those birds, that they,
like us, are carrying on, you
from whatever perch you have
come to rest on, me still here,
where I see you unexpectedly
appear in an Easter lily, in the shape
of my daughter's nose, in the high
meringue of a lemon pie set
in a restaurant window – how
I feel you unfold in these unspooled
notes, and even though you are
nowhere here, for a moment you are
where my husband, trying
to comfort me, promised me
you would be, everywhere—

Thirteen Ways of Looking at a Lemon

after Wallace Stevens

I
Out of the last hard ground,
A sprout thrust itself.
A lemon was born.

II
I placed four, no seven, lemons
In a bowl for
Evenness.

III
The sour lemon lay on the yellow pillow.
A thin outline of the whole.

IV
A lemon
Is helpful.
A lemon and some sugar and some ice
Is helpful.

V
I sliced the lemon for my water each morning
In thin, papery sluices
Or in thick wedges
One without and one with edges
Both with juices.

VI
Fish stared at me from the deli case
With sharp jagged ices
Little lemon sunshines lay around their heads
Halos or balloons
The floating
Over the fish and the cold
Made the crisis melt away.

VII

O women of Whole Foods
Why do you pucker picking among the fruits?
Can't you see how the lemon
Is more a womb than vacuum
With eyeless embryo seeds?

VIII

Meat has no meter
There is no beat in its sinews
But the lemon makes meter
And the meeting is involved
In the meter it makes.

IX

When the last lemons are squeezed,
The pulp, the rind, the remaining pith
Still sit on the countertop.

X

A lemon falling into a pond
Making a small plip;
Even the glassy surface of the water
Ripple would create a wake.

XI

She walked through the California fields
In canvas shoes.
Twice images leapt between the trees,
One was the sinking sun
And one was a large lemon
Falling into the horizon.

XII

The beer is bubbling.
The lemon must be listening.

XIII
The fruit was still in the painting.
It was yellow paint
That made the fruit seem yellow.
The lemon wilted
Between the leaving and the leaves.

My Mother, Murderess

Dripping in moonlight,
my mother: murderess,
hauls out the watering can
stuffed full. Deliberately
she covers each snail
with a mealy trickle
of salt. They boil up
into the dark, soapy
and destroyed, all snail moil
and ooze—

From the gut stained sidewalk,
we can hear them wail—

Triumphant in the morning,
on the lemony kitchen table,
she spoons out strawberries—
exact and uneaten.

Squash

My mother, who is not the squeamish kind,
does not wear lipstick, doesn't twist her hair,
wears mother bras and mother underwear;
and often in her garden you will find
her planted, when her arm begins to wind,
and suddenly she pitches out from there—
a snail. It hits the pavement, cracks, her stare
is steely in the starlit yard that's vined
and weedless. Night lies thick against the squash
she's saved. She walks inside, begins to wash
the soil from her hands with lemon soap.
Its bright scent drifts a moment, and I hope
that after I am kissed and tucked in bed,
she'll go outside—make sure that it's dead.

Beets

Skins thick and shaggy yield to slough away
under the carving. Blade amasses juice,
glossed with phosphorescence until a sluice
of water washes knife, aims to allay
beet's grip. Fingers know the pigments stay
for hours. My hand stands one in its noose
of flesh. The pieces fall with want to loose
themselves from whole, swirled insides on display.
My grandmother pared beets to make a borscht,
the kitchen redolent of earth and sun;
she'd clean their bodies, snap them into parts,
leaf from root, then cut with quiet force.
The counter, evidenced with what she'd done—
scarlet bleeding, bright as thin, sliced hearts.

A Persimmon

October was persimmons
for my father's fruit-of-the-month club,
and because my grandmother was in hospice,

hooked up to the machinery of leaving,
and because we didn't know
what to make of the four days of waiting,

or of the orange fruit delivered
to his door, he brought one with him
to the hospital. We turned shifts,

ate sandwiches, listened to the unsettling
of her breath, the soft air hissing
into the hospital's mattress,

while the persimmon sat on the side table,
a curved luminary in a room where little
by little light was leaving. Leaving

the next morning, I took my father's
gift in my palm, the brightness of fruit
held together by skin,

carried it home, cut
into it—eight neat slices
and swallowed my sorrow.

I know how a persimmon tastes
after it has waited with a father
for someone adored to die—

the stiff flower of leaves sheltering
each top, all sweetness coalesced
in the flesh.

Worm Bin

Sunk into the soil of our yard, a worm
bin contains what's left of last night's
salad, lettuce wilting, sucked holey, decay
and worm castings. The worms weave
unaware of why

they twist, eyeless, instinctively turn
from sun. My daughters and I visit with apple
cores, crescents of bruised pear, eggshells,
seeded strawberries; a lush ritual where rot
turns over on itself,

and treed oranges, heavy, still green,
sway. In Sanskrit their name means fragrant,
naranja, but worms have no noses. On some
trees the fruit stays lime-green all year long.
Already the orange

orange is decaying. Death and the living
sing to each other, squirm,
squint away light, food scraps,
binned endings
and beginnings.

Our own molecules too soon turn
wilted leaf, peeled orange. One daughter
tells us worms have five hearts.
We are hesitating
to put the lid back on.

Mangos

We buy mangos with expectations—
already taste the flower-sweet

juice on our tongues. Their green-
orange swirled skins speckled

from being Earth-bound, heavy
with juice, waiting, wind.

My husband takes the knife,
positions it off-center and glides

down each side, crisscrossing
steel through sugar, like a fish

through water. Then, folding
each side out, the yolk-gold

flesh arching, he releases it
into porcelain bowls. It's best

eaten like this, spoon and sunlight
in the early quiet of a new day,

the creamed coffee still steaming
from our cups, the blue

stretch of sky like a new skin,
ripe and waiting to be lived in—

The Request

Please make bread for me when I am gone.
Wake the yeast in a navy bowl, pour

the water in a thin stream until each granule
twists its grainy body, breathes, eats

its ration of sugar. Please use eggs to make
the loaf light-yellow, add their center suns

one by one, throw a pinch of salt over
your shoulder, leave the butter on the counter

like my mother did. Add the flour all at once,
so that its fog falls onto the counter top.

When you knead, push into the dough
any residue of anger, drink hot tea

and read while you pause for everything
to rise. Be patient. The loaf is legless

and will wait. Bake our bread, watching
the howl of steam coil up from the cuts

you have sliced into its top, remove it
from the oven like a small, wild animal.

Use a serrated knife—no—tear
the brief crust, push the tender inside

to your lips. Eat the miracle
we have made, I from the grave, you

from the kitchen, grateful I was once alive
to tell you this—grateful you are living.

Acknowledgements

I am grateful to the editors of the following publications for previously publishing some of these poems and/or other work: *Rattle, Poetry Super Highway, Riprap, Lipstick Party Magazine, indicia, Poets Reading the News, Mothers Always Write, Tuck Magazine, Modern Loss, Dissident Voice, Southeast Review Online, Modern Loss, f(r)iction, The Poet's Billow, Foothill Literary Journal, TAB: The Journal of Poetry & Poetics, Shrew, Rise Up Review, The Museum of Americana, Manzano Mountain Review, Thimble Literary Magazine, catheXis northwest press, Cultural Weekly, Medusa's Laugh Press, Connotation Press, The A3 Review, The New Limestone Review, Spectrum,* the San Gabriel Valley Poetry Festival, *The Fox Poetry Box,* and *Mezzo Cammin.*

***

I would like to acknowledge and thank the following people: my family; University of California, Santa Barbara English professor emeritus and poet John Ridland; the faculty at California State University, Long Beach, especially Charles Harper Webb, Bill Mohr, Patty Seyburn, David Hernandez, Suzanne Greenburg, Lisa Glatt, George Hart, and Mark Williams; poets Suzanne Lummis, Donna Hilbert, Armine Iknadossian, Lois P. Jones, Sonia Greenfield, and Alexis Rhone Fancher, Jenn Bakulin, the editors and readers at *Palette Poetry,* the "rengagades": Carolyn Estrada, Lorna Adkins, and Stephanie Miller, artist Anglie Rehnberg, photographer, Sheri DiPietro, and publisher and poet Eric Morago.

About the Author

Alexandra Umlas is a Pushcart Prize and Best of the Net nominated poet. You can find her work in *Rattle, Connotation Press, Poetry Super Highway, Cultural Weekly, Foothill Journal, and New Limestone Review,* among others. Her honors include first place in the *F(r)iction* Poetry Contest (2017), the *Southeast Review's* Writer's Regimen Contest (2017), the *Poetry Super Highway* Poetry Contest (2018), and the Tom Park Poetry Prize from the *Fox Poetry Box* (2019). She serves as a reader for *Palette Poetry* and on the board of directors of Tebot Bach. She holds an M.F.A. in Poetry from California State University, Long Beach and an M.Ed. in Cross-cultural Education. Born in Long Beach, CA she currently lives in Huntington Beach, CA with her husband and two daughters. www.alexandraumlas.com

Patrons

Moon Tide Press would like to thank the following people for their support in helping publish the finest poetry from the Southern California region. To sign up as a patron, visit www.moontidepress.com or send an email to publisher@moontidepress.com.

Anonymous
Robin Axworthy
Conner Brenner
Bill Cushing
Susan Davis
Peggy Dobreer
Dennis Gowans
Alexis Rhone Fancher
Half Off Books & Brad T. Cox
Jim & Vicky Hoggatt
Ron Koertge & Bianca Richards
Ray & Christi Lacoste
Zachary & Tammy Locklin
Lincoln McElwee
David McIntire
José Enrique Medina
Andrew November
Michael Miller & Rachanee Srisavasdi
Terri Niccum
Ronny & Richard Morago
Jennifer Smith
Andrew Turner
Mariano Zaro

Also Available from Moon Tide Press

The Book of Rabbits, Vince Trimboli (2019)

Everything I Write Is a Love Song to the World, David McIntire (2019)

Letters to the Leader, HanaLena Fennel (2019)

Darwin's Garden, Lee Rossi (2019)

Dark Ink: A Poetry Anthology Inspired by Horror (2018)

Drop and Dazzle, Peggy Dobreer (2018)

Junkie Wife, Alexis Rhone Fancher (2018)

The Moon, My Lover, My Mother, & the Dog, Daniel McGinn (2018)

Lullaby of Teeth: An Anthology of Southern California Poetry (2017)

Angels in Seven, Michael Miller (2016)

A Likely Story, Robbi Nester (2014)

Embers on the Stairs, Ruth Bavetta (2014)

The Green of Sunset, John Brantingham (2013)

The Savagery of Bone, Timothy Matthew Perez (2013)

The Silence of Doorways, Sharon Venezio (2013)

Cosmos: An Anthology of Southern California Poetry (2012)

Straws and Shadows, Irena Praitis (2012)

In the Lake of Your Bones, Peggy Dobreer (2012)

I Was Building Up to Something, Susan Davis (2011)

Hopeless Cases, Michael Kramer (2011)

One World, Gail Newman (2011)

What We Ache For, Eric Morago (2010)

Now and Then, Lee Mallory (2009)

Pop Art: An Anthology of Southern California Poetry (2009)

In the Heaven of Never Before, Carine Topal (2008)

A Wild Region, Kate Buckley (2008)

Carving in Bone: An Anthology of Orange County Poetry (2007)

Kindness from a Dark God, Ben Trigg (2007)

A Thin Strand of Lights, Ricki Mandeville (2006)

Sleepyhead Assassins, Mindy Nettifee (2006)

Tide Pools: An Anthology of Orange County Poetry (2006)

Lost American Nights: Lyrics & Poems, Michael Ubaldini (2006)